# A World Adrift

## South China Sea to Inner Mongolia

For *A World Adrift* Unknown Fields travel through Asia and beyond, tracing the shadows of the world's desires and along the supply chains and cargo routes of the South China Sea to explore the dispersed choreographies and atomised geographies that the globalised city brings into being. These are the contours of our distributed city, stretched around the earth from the hole in the ground to the high street shelf.

In a world of bytes and bitcoins, cyberspace and clouds, 90% of the world's cargo still travels by sea. It is not beamed or teleported or conjured into existence along strings of fibre optics but dragged across the planet in heaving steel mega ships full of glistening gadgets, plastic toys and gizmos from distant lands. Consignments of the precious and industrial, raw and refined, mechanical and living, drift across infrastructural seas suspended in maritime space on vast Panamax, Aframax and Suezmax and traded in wholesale markets the size of cities. The secret lives of objects span across a notional factory floor stretching from the high street 99cent shop all the way to the resource fields of the Far East.

This book is a collection of conversations and overheard chatter from Unknown Fields' journey along the city's supply chain. From sea to source, we follow the routes of bits, bobs and thingamajigs in reverse and chart their unmaking, from container ship back through wholesalers and manufacturers and ending at the banks of the sludge-filled radioactive lake in Inner Mongolia where some of these objects begin their journey. Our cities are extraordinary constellations of products, goods and technologies. From the smallest and most inconsequential of objects to the most intricate and complex, these material things set in motion this vast, planetary scale infrastructure. Our city casts shadows that stretch far and wide.

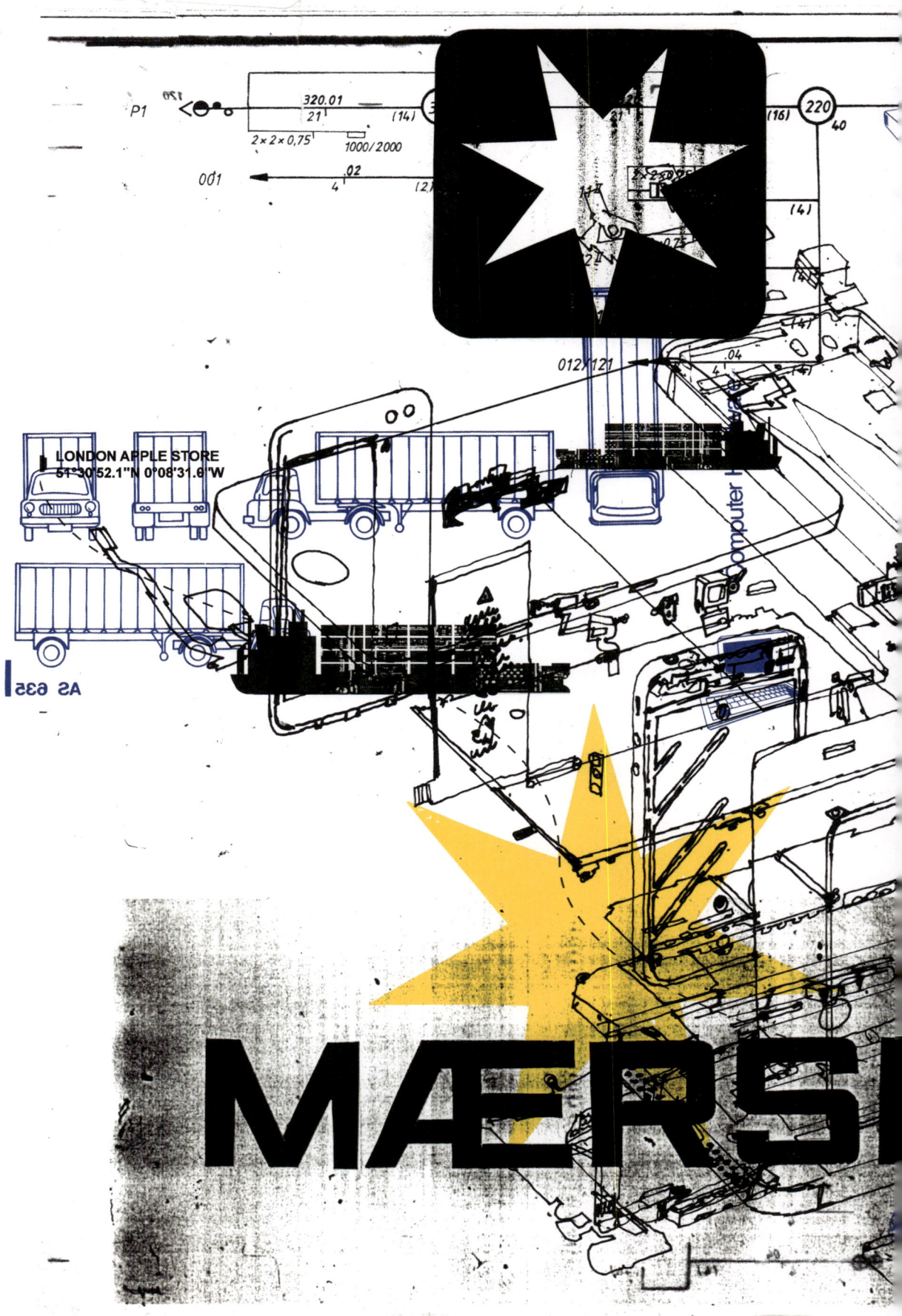

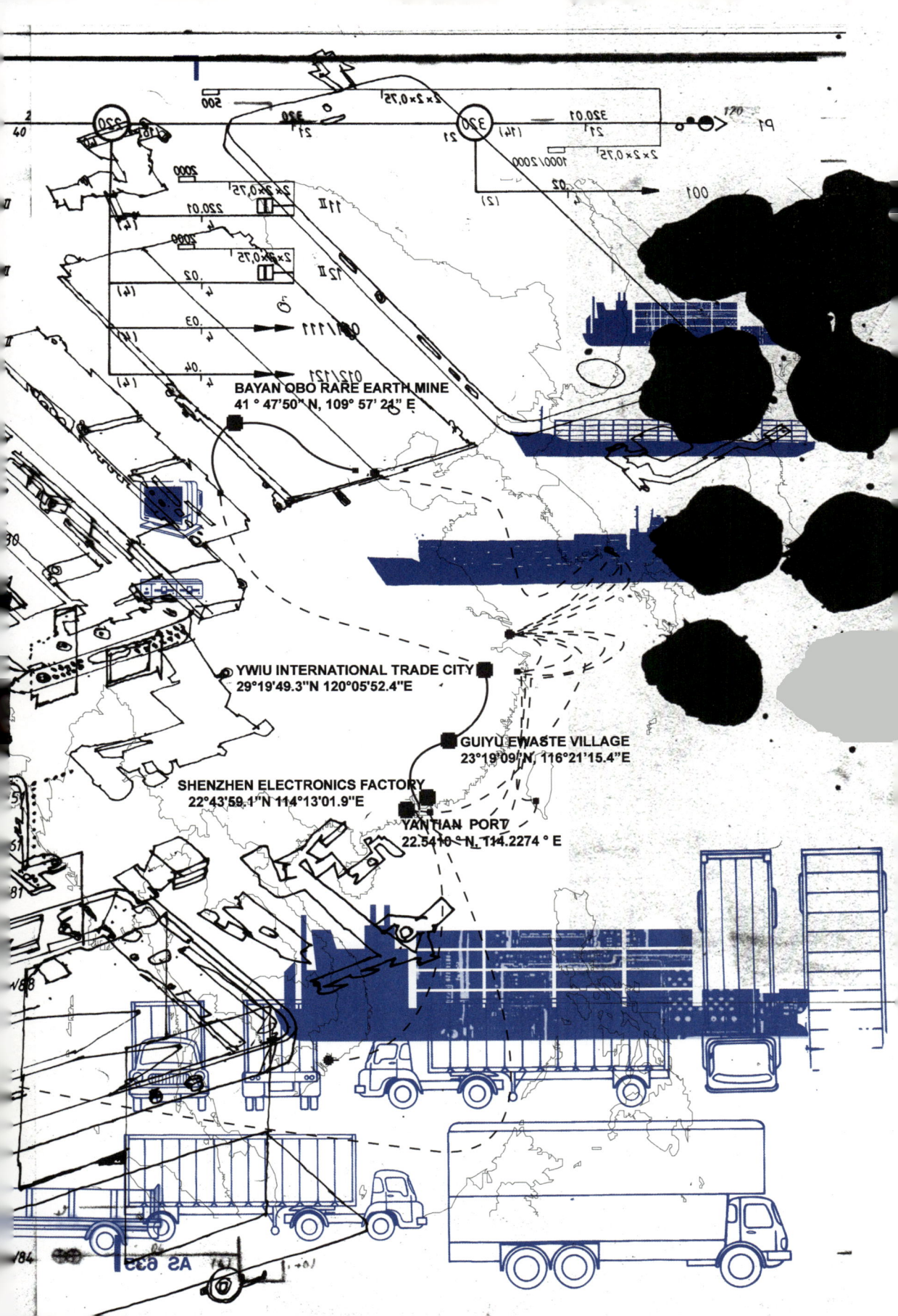

BAYAN OBO RARE EARTH MINE
41 ° 47'50" N, 109° 57' 21" E

YWIU INTERNATIONAL TRADE CITY
29°19'49.3"N 120°05'52.4"E

GUIYU EWASTE VILLAGE
23°19'09"N, 116°21'15.4"E

SHENZHEN ELECTRONICS FACTORY
22°43'59.1"N 114°13'01.9"E

YANTIAN PORT
22.5410 ° N, 114.2274 ° E

# THE INVISIBLE NETWORK

IT'S BEEN JUST OVER 45 YEARS SINCE THE APOLLO MOON LANDINGS,
AND SOME WOULD HAVE IT THAT WE ARE FAILING TO BUILD BIG ANYMORE.
STAND ON THE BRIDGE OF A CONTAINER SHIP DOCKED IN A MEGA-PORT
IN KOREA, HOWEVER, AND IT'S CLEAR THIS IS JUST NOT TRUE.
Text fragments chronicling our journey by Unknown Fields
Embedded Journalist, Tim Maughan

# 35 06' 20.7" N 129° 02' 31.9" E

While no one was watching the world has built
a continuous conveyor belt stretching across
the globe that is formed from an ever-shifting
constellation of containers, ships the size of
buildings, dislocated factory floors and vast
excavated landscapes.

NET
GLOBAL 5000
3.6

# 3.6 MILLION CONTAINERS ARE IN MOTION WORLDWIDE

 In a world of bytes and bitcoins, cyberspace and clouds, 90% of the world's cargo still travels by sea.

# 5,000 SHIPS MAKE UP THE GLOBAL CONTAINERSHIP FLEET

**NAME: GUNHILDE MAERSK**
**IMO: 9359026**
**MMSI: 220595000**
**TYPE: CONTAINER SHIP**
**CAPACITY: 9,000 containers**
**GROSS TON: 98268**
**SUM DWT: 116100t**
**BUILD: 2008**
**FLAG: DENMARK INTERNATIONAL REGISTER**

NET
21.960

AS 635

Soon we're into the depths of Busan Port,
and speeding past endless, towering stacks of
shipping containers until we're finally dwarfed
by the huge blue mass of the *Maersk Seletar*,
the 320m-long, 80,000 tonne, 9,000 container-
capacity ship that will be our home for the
next seven days.
**TM**

'We head from here in China to South Africa, then back to east Asia to refuel in
Singapore, then South America, Russia and back to China before doing it all again.
One global circuit on our ship takes 4.5 months.'
Chief engineer, *Maersk Seletar*

CRANE AND TRUCK DRIVERS ARE LITTLE MORE THAN ELEMENTS IN A VAST
ROBOTIC SYSTEM, RECEIVING INSTRUCTIONS FROM THE ALGORITHMS OF
MAERSK'S VAST GLOBAL COMPUTER NETWORK, FOLLOWING ORDERS ON ENDLESS
CYCLES UNTIL THEIR SHIFTS END.
TM

# 8.860 KGS NET
# 10.160 KGS

Arriving into port at night we are presented
with a nightmarish, *Blade Runner*-esque landscape
of glowing lights and smokestacks painting the
low cloud ceiling orange. You not only see the
pollution - the vast carbon footprint of this
industrial network - but taste it in the air.
It's easy to forget how much of that impact
the Chinese people are taking as a direct hit
themselves, as much for the west's benefit as
their own.
**TM**

AX.G
CHINA

PORTS

# 7 OF THE 10 BUSIEST CONTAINER PORTS ARE IN CHINA

The surfaces of our planet's oceans – for centuries a space of mystery and myth, of expanse and desolation – have been rationalised. Once an enigmatic, awe-inspiring place, the sea has become a zone of efficiency, little more than another channel for the automated supply-chain network.
**TM**

'Years ago, when we would travel through warmer waters we would see an enormous amount of wildlife. The sea used to be filled with phosphorescent algae that would glow when the waters were disturbed. We would leave this luminous green trail behind us as the propellers churned up the algae. Toilets are flushed with seawater and you could turn the lights off in the bathroom and flush the loo and the whole room would glow neon green.'
**Captain Brian Argent,** *Maersk Seletar*

Over the course of seven days there wasn't a
single time when I stood on the bridge of the
*Seletar*, even when deep at sea, that I couldn't
look out and see other container ships, and a
brief scan of the horizon with binoculars would
usually reveal four or five more.

      The sea has become dominated by GPS
tracking and autopiloted navigation, where
the shipping routes are more than just vague
geographical gestures, but instead precise
spaces traced out both by computerised charts
and physical markers, with deep-sea buoys marking
lanes like the painted lines on road surfaces.
**TM**

'You don't talk to other ships anymore. Many years ago each ship used to have three reel-to-reel movies per month. When you were in port you would swap these with other ships. Now we just have Netflix.'
**Captain Brian Argent,** *Maersk Seletar*

# NOBODY ON THE SHIP KNOWS WHAT LIES INSIDE THE CONTAINERS IT CARRIES

'There was a container ship that broke in two off the coast of the UK. It was carrying containers full of cars. A few days later, as the containers washed up on shore, everyone nearby was able to start driving around in BMWs. It takes an event like this for us to get a glimpse into this hidden system.'
**Captain Brian Argent,** *Maersk Seletar*

There are exceptions of course; only hazardous
materials travelling in containers must be
declared, as must the contents of the refrigerated
containers - known in the industry as reefers.
The reefers themselves are fascinating pieces
of technology, basic containers outfitted to be
advanced climate-controlled, computer-monitored
micro-environments. Checking the reefers are
running is the crew's only tangible, direct
responsibility for the cargo beyond ensuring
it arrives on time. Even so, it is still highly
computer-controlled; the ship's captain, Brian
Argent, tells me that the crew's emails piggy-back
off a satellite uplink designed to keep an eye on
the reefers, transmitting status updates thousands
of miles back to land so that the company's
computers know about a problem even before the
ship's crew.

**TM**

We are only part of the supply chain. We don't see what's going on behind the scenes most of the time. We are on the ship, we arrive into port, the cargo is loaded, we leave port, we go to the next port and the cargo is discharged. We don't know where they have come from, what's in them or where they were filled. The boxes are just loaded on and off. At the moment we are in autopilot and although I am monitoring whats going on I am not using my skills.'

**Captain Brian Argent,** *Maersk Seletar*

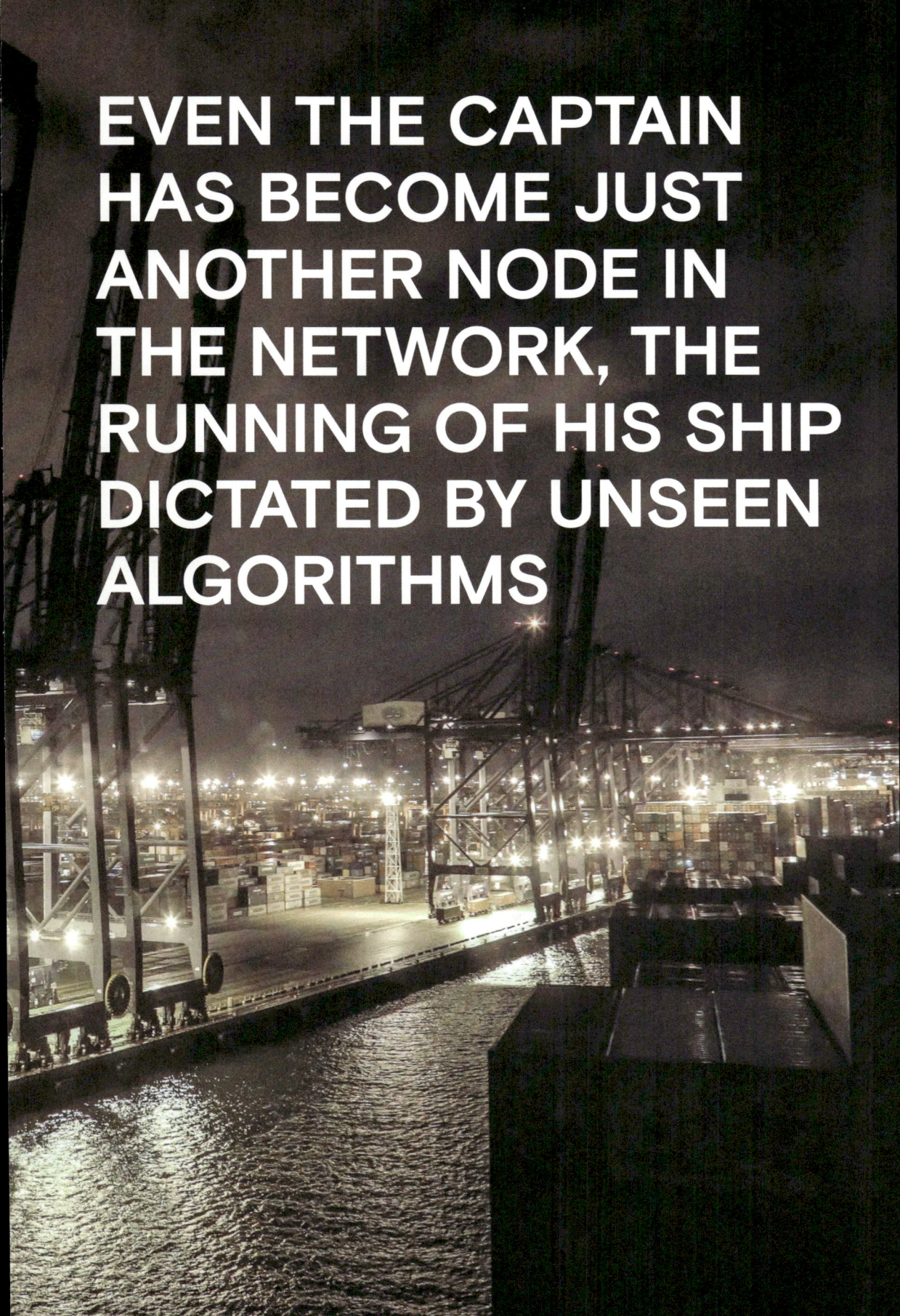

EVEN THE CAPTAIN HAS BECOME JUST ANOTHER NODE IN THE NETWORK, THE RUNNING OF HIS SHIP DICTATED BY UNSEEN ALGORITHMS

# 22°
# 34'
# 25.7"
# N
# 114°
# 15'
# 56.4"
# E

'Do you think the general public ever thinks about you when they go into the shop and buy the latest iPhone? If you have ever bought something it has probably come out of a container.'
Captain Brian Argent, *Maersk Seletar*

The *Maersk Seletar* is just another node in the network, another rationalised point in the global infrastructure, a bridge between the physical and digital. Once I realised this, I knew it was time to abandon my romantic notions of being away at sea, that it was pointless to resist the lure of the network, and found myself squatting in the stairwell between decks C and D, trying to get reconnected.
**TM**

'This ship is called the *New Dream*. It is almost finished.'
SWS shipyard welder

# CHINA IS THE LARGEST SHIPBUILDING NATION IN THE WORLD

31°
20'
06.1'
N
121°
38'
05.5"
E

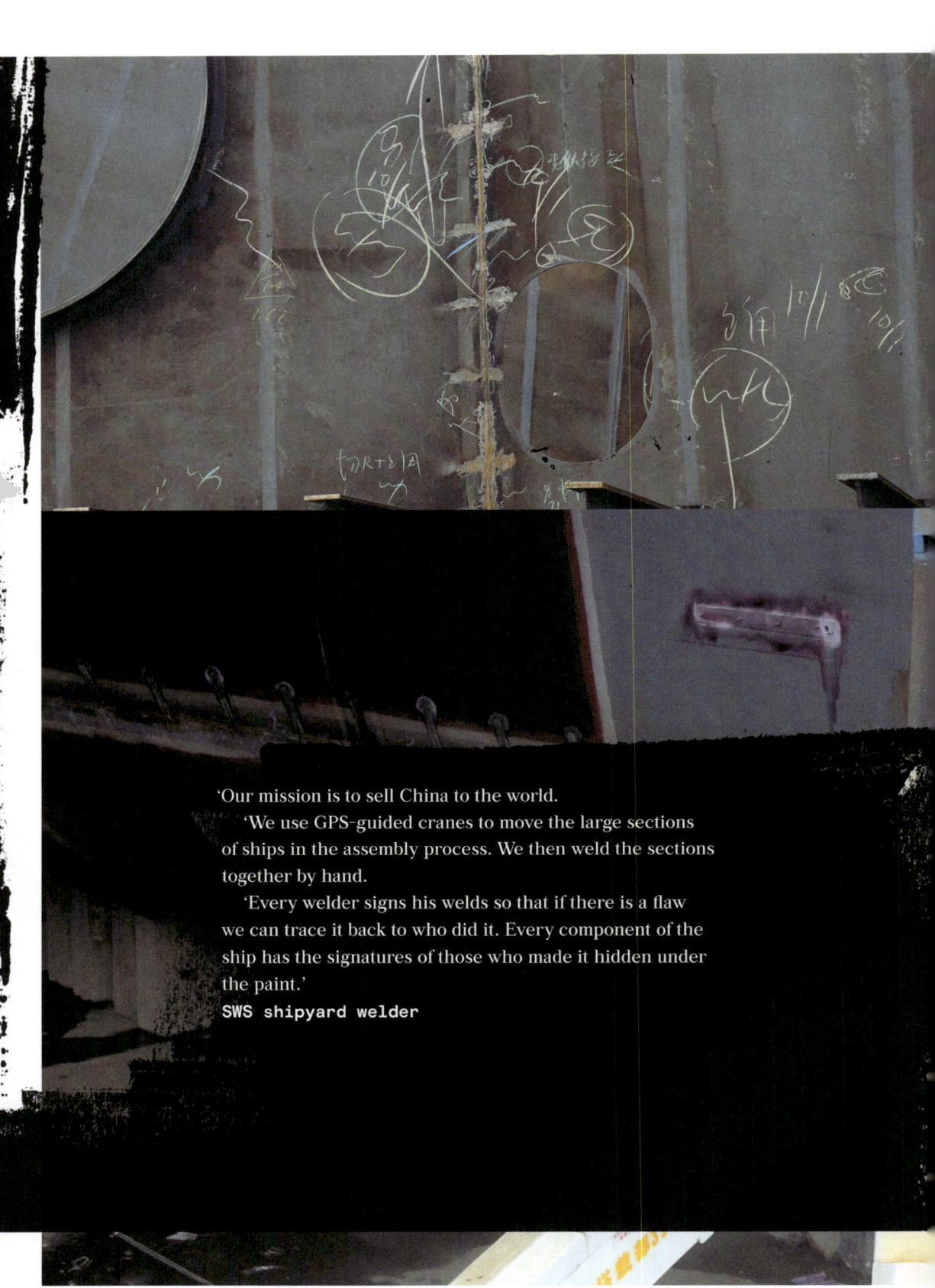

'Our mission is to sell China to the world.
'We use GPS-guided cranes to move the large sections of ships in the assembly process. We then weld the sections together by hand.
'Every welder signs his welds so that if there is a flaw we can trace it back to who did it. Every component of the ship has the signatures of those who made it hidden under the paint.'
**SWS shipyard welder**

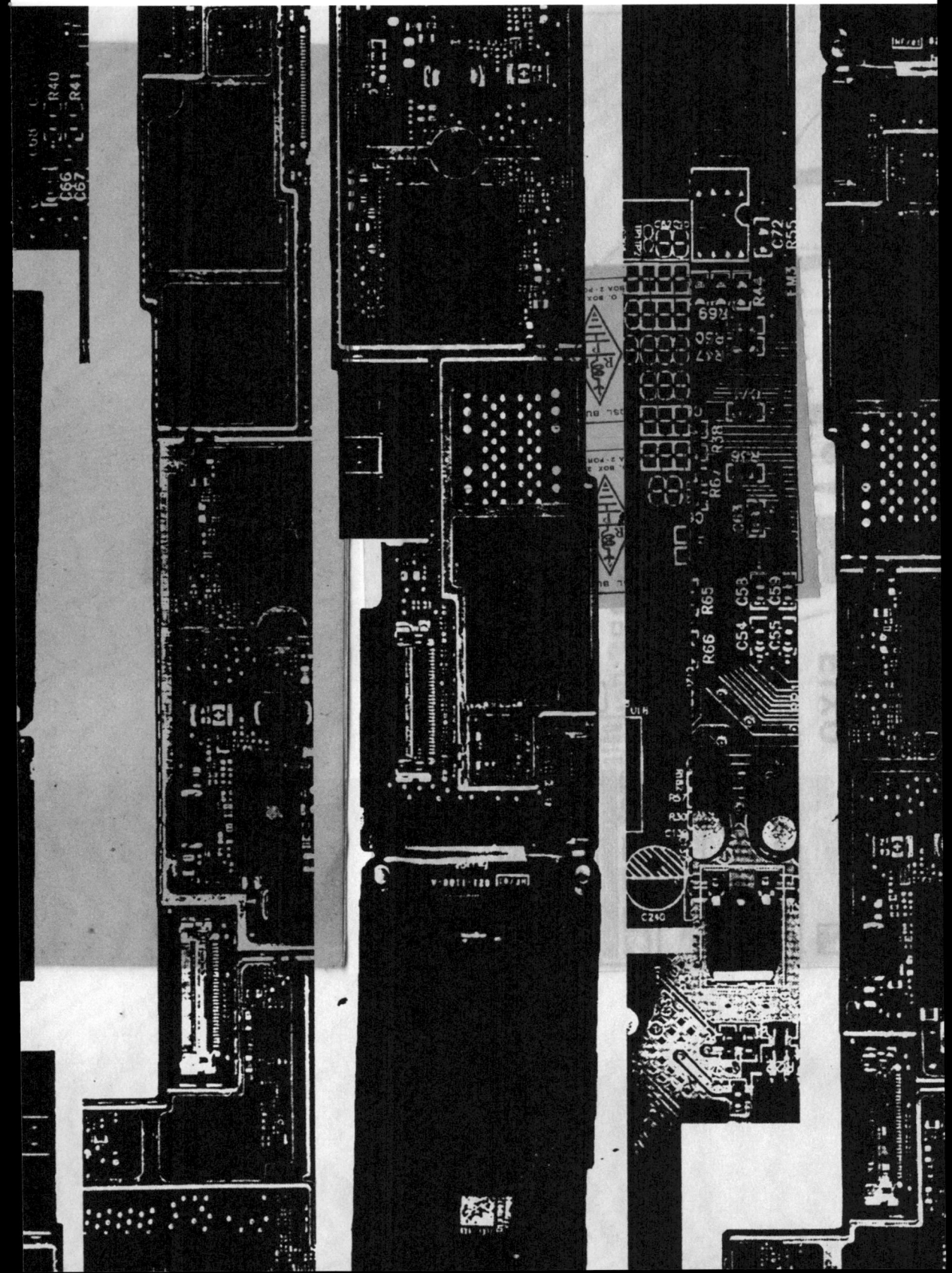

THE WHOLESALE CITY CONSISTS OF 80,000 SHOPS, ALL IDENTICALLY SIZED
2.5M BY 2.5M CUBES CONTAINING 10 MILLION PRODUCTS STRETCHED ACROSS
10 SQUARE KILOMETRES.

# 1,000 CONTAINERS A DAY ARE SHIPPED FROM YIWU WHOLESALE CITY

29°
19'
48.4"
N

120°
06'

BEFORE OBJECTS SET SAIL FOR OUR STORES THEY ARE BOUGHT, SOLD AND TRADED IN THE VAST HALLS OF YIWU INTERNATIONAL TRADE CITY, A WHOLESALE MARKET THE SIZE OF A CITY.

The market has its own inland port where it loads the world's containers. It's an international customs zone suspended like an island, free from the jurisdiction of the surrounding Zhejiang Province.
TM

The market is less a shopping mall than a vast,
endless trade show, built for the most important
of middlemen: retail buyers who flock here
from across China and the rest of the world
to negotiate deals on shipping containers full
of cheap products to fill the shelves of stores
back home.

I've not seen daylight for over three
hours. I'm also hopelessly lost. I've been trying
to get out of this place for the last 45 minutes,
but the vast labyrinth of corridors and stores
all look identical.
**TM**

'Sorry we can't do it, my minimum order is 100,000.'
**Yiwu market trader**

WE UNDERSTAND
WHO WE ARE
THROUGH
THE TRAIL OF
OBJECTS WE
LEAVE BEHIND

**THE PHYSICAL MANIFESTATION OF THE VAST INVISIBLE NETWORK THAT SUPPLIES ALL OF THE INEXPENSIVE GOODS WE ALL BUY IN THE WEST.**

It's the little items that fill your desk drawers; the free pens that salesmen give you, and the toys your children break or forget. It's the hundreds of disposable products that fill 99cent stores and gas stations. It's the stuff you buy on impulse, or because it's momentarily funny. And all because it's cheap. China is the global leader in creating plastic junk, and Yiwu market is its showroom.

More than 60% of the world's Christmas decorations are made in Yiwu, a significant proportion of which is sold at this enormous wholesale market. Christmas is made in Yiwu. That tree lighting up your lounge. Those decorations hanging from the ceiling. That novelty stocking filler you bought for your child. Chances are they came not far from where I am standing.

**TM**

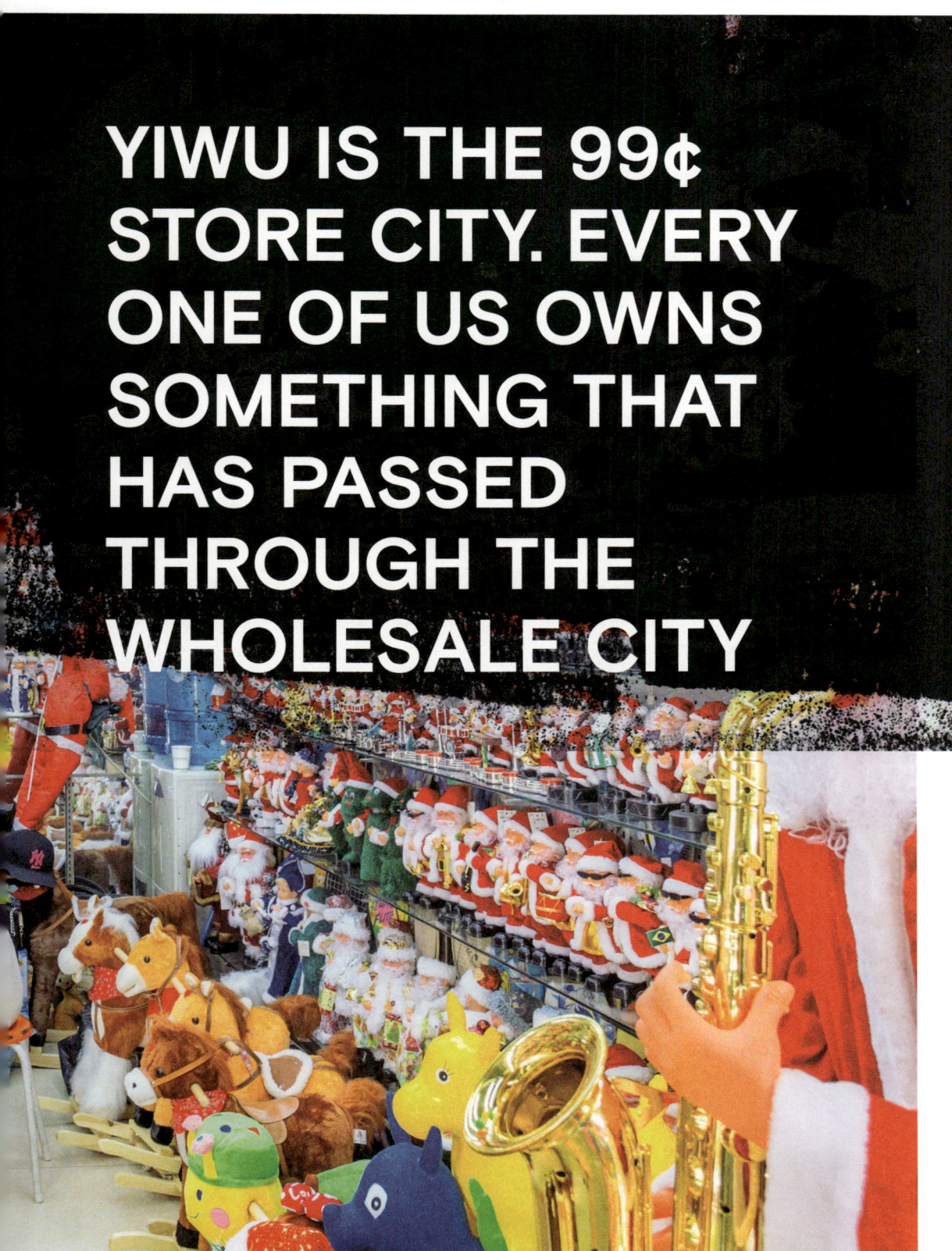

# YIWU IS THE 99¢ STORE CITY. EVERY ONE OF US OWNS SOMETHING THAT HAS PASSED THROUGH THE WHOLESALE CITY

# Yiwu Hangtian Arts & Crafts Factory

I watch a girl sew white fur trim onto red felt
at the rate of about two hats a minute, and as
she finishes one she simply pushes it off the
front of her desk where they fall, silently,
onto an ever increasing pile on the floor.

Upstairs is the plastic moulding room,
mainly staffed by young men, stripped to the
waist because of the heat. The air here is
thick with fumes, the smell of chemicals and
warm plastic. The men feed plastic pellets from
Samsung-branded sacks into machines to be melted
down, and then pressed into moulds to make toy
snowmen and Father Christmases. It's repetitive,
and potentially dangerous, as the workers must
constantly reach inside the large presses.
**TM**

29°
11'
18.5"
N
120°
02'
37.6"
E

# SHENZHEN MAKES 90% OF THE WORLD'S ELECTRONICS

43' 59.1" N 114° 13' 01.9" E

A gadget no longer exists as a singular object in a pocket or on a desk. Every object we own has resonate effects and is atomised across a factory floor that extends from the high street shop to the production infrastructures of the far east. We can't think of our cities as single points on a map anymore.

# A PLANETARY-SCALED CONVEYOR BELT

The truth here is actually the real secret of China's manufacturing success – keeping labour costs so low that making things by hand is cheaper than using machines.

Many of them pass the time while they work watching Chinese TV dramas on the very smartphones that they are making.

**TM**

THESE ARE THE HUMAN MACHINES OF THE PRODUCTION LINE, ALL CHOREOGRAPHED BY EFFICIENCY ALGORITHMS AND THEIR BODIES MATCHED IN SPEED TO THE CONVEYOR IN FRONT OF THEM. THESE ARE THE REAL ROBOTS OF OUR CITIES OF TECHNOLOGY.

GUANGDONG PROVINCE HOSTS AN ESTIMATED 60,000
FACTORIES AND 10 MILLION RURAL MIGRANT WORKERS.

'All our buildings are connected with conveyor belts. The
factory never ends and it never stops rolling. 24 hours a day.'
TCL television factory manager

THE CITY IS A NETWORKED LANDSCAPE CAUGHT WITHIN THE EVER-
SHIFTING TANGLES OF SUPPLY LINES AND SHIPPING LANES AND
CRAFTED FROM INVISIBLE CONNECTIONS AND HIDDEN RELATIONSHIPS.

People and spaces ignored or forgotten behind the gloss of the screen, the seamless aluminum edge or the glare of the pixel.

Could we imagine redesigning our gadgets not based on how they slide into our pocket or feel in our hand but for the networks they set in motion or the economic resources they might distribute? What could the alternative design criteria be for supply-chain design if they weren't engineered around cheap labour costs and material availability?

'We have seen on our cameras that you have been taking photos. We cannot let you leave until we see that you have all deleted your hard drives.'
**TCL public relations officer**

# Guiyu e-Waste Village

A VILLAGE ORGANISED AROUND METALS AND HARDWARE COMPONENTS.
DISTRICTS OF RARE EARTH MAGNETS EXTRACTION, PRECINCTS OF
COPPER SMELTING.

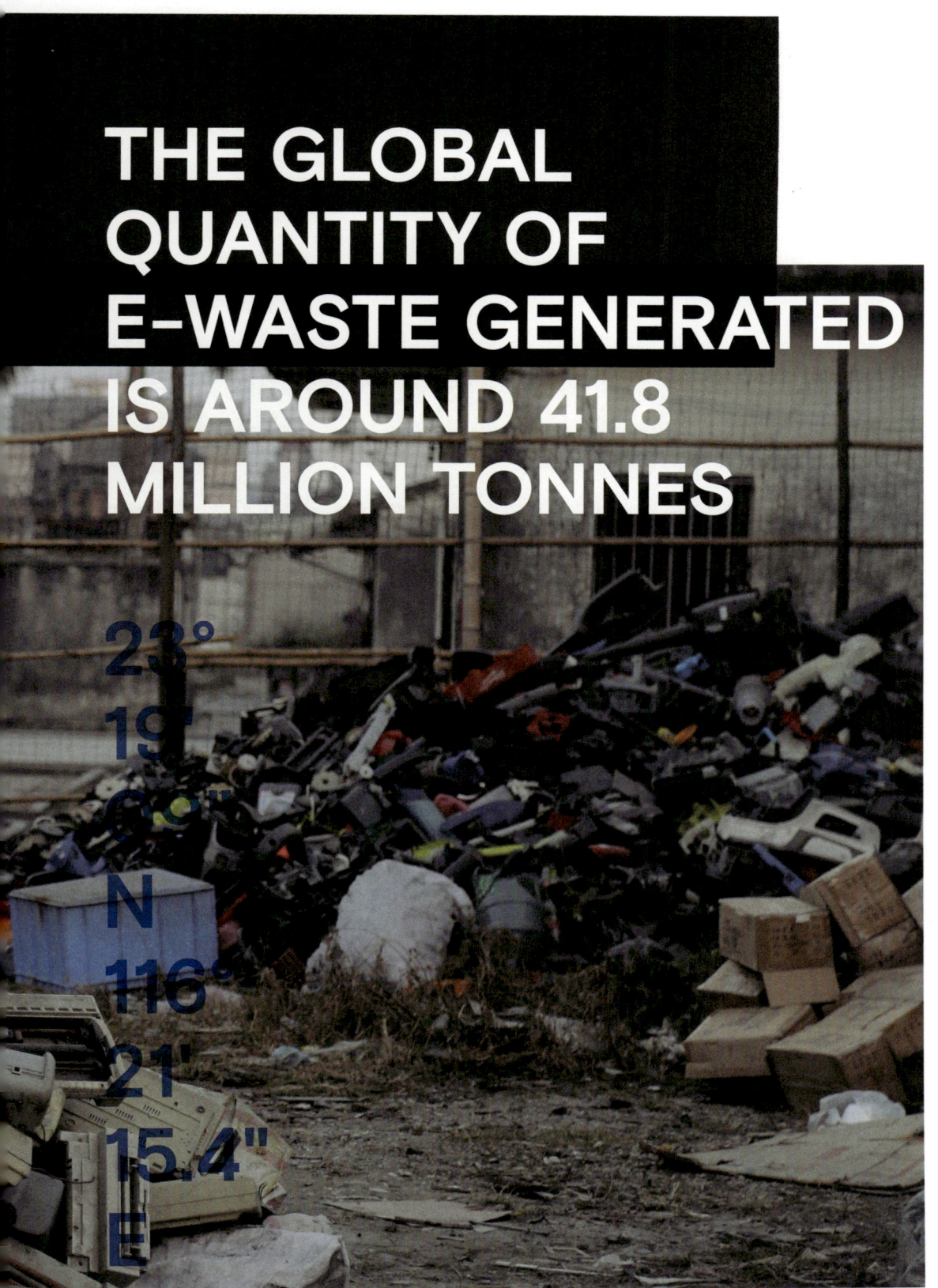

# THE GLOBAL QUANTITY OF E-WASTE GENERATED IS AROUND 41.8 MILLION TONNES

The inhabitants of Guiyu collect the e-waste
in their houses, surrounding their living,
sleeping and eating spaces. Mining their domestic
landscapes for lead, germanium, gallium, tin,
nickel and copper.
        Now kitchens and living rooms are mine
sites. Next to the pot of noodles simmers
the acid bath, dissolving circuit wafers and
separating metals and flavouring soup.

THESE ARE THE
REAL DIGITAL
NATIVES
OF THE CITY

# Baotou Refinery Tailings Lake

CHINA PRODUCES OVER 95% OF THE WORLD'S RARE EARTH'S MINERALS.
TWO THIRDS OF THIS IS IN BAOTOU.

# 3,000 TONNES OF RARE EARTH METALS USED IN HARD DRIVES

From where I'm standing, the city-sized Baogang Steel and Rare Earth complex dominates the horizon, its endless cooling towers and chimneys reaching up into grey, washed-out sky. Between it and me, stretching into the distance, lies an artificial lake filled with a black, barely liquid, toxic sludge. Welcome to Baotou, the largest industrial city in Inner Mongolia.

You may not have heard of Baotou, but the mines and factories here help to keep our modern lives ticking. It is one of the world's biggest suppliers of 'rare earth' minerals. These elements can be found in everything from magnets in wind turbines and electric car motors, to the electronic guts of smartphones and flatscreen TVs.

At night, multicoloured lights, glass dyed by rare earth elements, line the larger roads, turning the city into a scene from *Tron*, while the smaller side streets are filled with drunk, vomiting refinery workers that spill from bars and barbecue joints.

At times it's impossible to tell where the vast structure of the Baogang refineries complex ends and the city begins.

Everywhere you look is a forest of flame-tipped refinery towers and endless electricity pylons. The air is filled with a constant, ambient smell of sulphur. It's the kind of industrial landscape that America and Europe have largely forgotten – at one time parts of Detroit or Sheffield must have looked and smelled like this.

**TM**

**WE BRAND OUR TECHNOLOGIES WITH TERMS LIKE CLOUD, AIR AND FEATHERWEIGHT BUT IN REALITY THEY ARE VIOLENTLY WRENCHED FROM THE EARTH.**

40°
49'08"
N
109°
40'
41.67"
E

Earlier reports claim the lake is guarded by the military, but we see no sign. We pass a shack that was presumably a guard post at one point but it's abandoned now; whoever was here left in a hurry, leaving their bedding, cooking stove, and instant noodle packets.

As I watched Apple announce their smart watch recently, a thought crossed my mind: once we made watches with minerals mined from the earth and treated them like precious heirlooms; now we use even rarer minerals to produce the latest-generation smart watches and we'll be urged to upgrade them each year.

Unsure of quite how to react, I take photos and shoot video on my cerium polished iPhone.

**TM**

# Baotou Toxicology Results: Rare Earth Mine

10 SQ KM MINE TAILINGS WASTE LAKE FILLED WITH A COCKTAIL
OF ACIDS, HEAVY METALS, CARCINOGENS AND RADIOACTIVE
MATERIAL ROUGHLY 3 TIMES BACKGROUND RADIATION.

While they're called rare earth minerals,
they're actually fairly common and quite evenly
distributed throughout the world's crust.
Arguably, what makes them scarce enough to be
profitable are the hugely hazardous and toxic
processes needed to extract them from ore and
to refine them into usable products It could
be argued that China's dominance of the rare
earth market is less about geology and far
more about the country's willingness to take
an environmental hit that other nations shy
away from.
**TM**

40 38'49.39"N – 109 40'41.67"E

# RARE EARTHEN WARE

NGP15003
dark grey fine (clay like)
mine tailings
40 38'48.48"N
– 109 40'39.20"E

– 109 40'41.67"E    – 109 40'41.45"E    – 109 40'39.20"E

| | | | | | |
|---|---|---|---|---|---|
| | <20 | | | | .2 |
| | <5 | | | | .8 |
| | 1330 | | | | 25 |
| | 4.6 | | | | .8 |
| Cadmium (Cd) | 2.6 | | 2.5 | 2.5 | 0.2 |
| | | | 27551 | 24005 | 60.0 |
| | | | 14 | 16 | 100 |
| | | | 28 | 9 | 25 |
| | | | 58 | 24 | 55 |
| Dy | | | 91 | 121 | 3.0 |
| Er | 43 | | 42.3 | 53.5 | 2.8 |
| Eu | | | 144 | 193 | 1.2 |
| Ga | | | 600 | 780 | 5 |
| Germanium (Ge) | <40 | | <40 | <40 | 1.5 |
| Holmium (Ho) | 11.5 | | 11.3 | 15.0 | 1.2 |
| Indium (In) | <10 | | <10 | <10 | 0.1 |
| Lanthanum (La) | 14936 | | 14913 | 20194 | 30.0 |
| Lead (Pb) | 556 | | 472 | 290 | 13 |
| Lutetium (Lu) | 1.1 | | 1.0 | 1.2 | 0.5 |
| Manganese (mn) | 7010 | | 7310 | 6175 | 950 |
| Mercury (Hg) | <20 | | <20 | <20 | 0.08 |
| Molybdenum (Mo) | 47.0 | | 39.9 | 72.4 | 1.5 |
| Neodymium (Nd) | 9917 | | 9317 | 11649 | 28.0 |
| Nickel (Ni) | 27.7 | | 27.7 | 12.9 | 75 |
| Niobium (Nb) | 302 | | 137 | 76 | 20 |
| Praseodymium (Pr) | 3013 | | 2851 | 3631 | 8.2 |
| Samarium (Sm) | 816 | | 778 | 1004 | 6.0 |
| Strontium | 443 | | 393 | 559 | 375 |
| Tantalum (Ta) | 9 | | 9 | 8 | 2 |
| Terbium (Tb) | 40.3 | | 39.9 | 51.8 | 0.9 |
| Thulium (Tm) | 1.7 | | 1.7 | 2.1 | 0.5 |
| Tungsten (W) | 20.3 | | 16.6 | 17.8 | 1.5 |
| Vanadium (V) | 26 | | 25 | 36 | 135 |
| Ytterbium (Yb) | 8.8 | | 8.8 | 10.6 | 3.4 |
| Yttrium (Y) | 139 | | 126 | 188 | 33 |
| Zinc (Zn) | 449 | | 530 | 375 | 70 |

From K.B. Kreuskopf & D.K. Bird (1994)
Introduction To Geochemistry, 3rd Edition.

"This sample is relatively high in a few key metals that are especially notorious for their toxicity to human, including Cadmium, Lead, Mercury, Arsenic and Chromium."

*Testing laboratory within Greenpeace, China.*

'Here we mainly produce cerium oxide which is used to polish
touchscreens on smartphones and tablets.'
**Baotou Rare Earth Refinery manager**

Rare Earth metals are the fundamental materials
that enable the 'featherweight', 'slim' and
'seamless' aesthetics of our contemporary
technologies. As our personal electronics tend
towards the invisible, they conjure in their
shadows an undeniably visible grey mountain,
a 1km deep pit, and a 10km radioactive
tailings lake, a counterweight to the apparent
immateriality of computing, communications and
electric energy.

Unknown Fields have used the toxic
mud from this tailings lake in Baotou, Inner
Mongolia to craft a set of three radioactive
ceramic vessels. The size of each vase is
determined by shaping it from the amount of
waste created in the production of three items
of technology – a smartphone, a featherweight
laptop and the cell of a smart car battery.
With a slightly shimmering burnish, from the
reaction of the mineral content during firing,
the vessels are the material shadow of valuable
technological object.

The toxic waste dug from this lake was
discharged from the surrounding factories and
contains a cocktail of acids, heavy metals,
carcinogens and radioactive material – including
thorium and uranium – used to process the 17
most sought-after minerals in the world, known
as rare earths. At the nearby Bayan Obo mine,
unpronounceable treasures – erbium, yttrium,
dysprosium, europium, neodymium – are drawn from
the 56 million tonne Treasure Mountain deposit;
the largest in the world.

In silhouette the vases echo highly
valuable Ming dynasty porcelain Tongping or
'Sleeve' vases. Ming vases are particularly
iconic objects of high value as well as being
artefacts of international trade. A one-family
global superpower, the Ming dynasty presided
over an international network of connections,
trade and diplomacy that stretched across Asia to
Africa, the Middle East and Europe, built on the
trade of commodities such as imperial porcelain.

These three 'rare earthenware' vessels
are the physical embodiment of a contemporary

WE SEE OURSELVES
REFLECTED IN THE
BLACK MIRRORS OF
OUR SCREENS AND
THE BLACK EARTH
OF OUR TOXIC LAKE

global supply network that displaces earth
and weaves matter across the planet. They
are presented as objects of desire, but their
elevated radiation levels and toxicity make
them objects we would not want to possess.
They represent the undesirable consequences
of our material desires.

    This book charts the unmaking of
these objects of technology — reversing their
journeys all the way back to a radioactive
lake in a remote landscape. The unmaking of
our technologies is the making of these vases,
carefully crafted from their toxic byproducts.

*A World Adrift* by Unknown Fields

Design: Neasden Control Centre & City Edition Studio
Illustration: Neasden Control Centre

Printed in Italy by Musumeci S.p.a.
ISBN 978-1-907896-86-6

For a catalogue of AA Publications visit
aaschool.ac.uk/publications or email publications@aaschool.ac.uk

AA Publications
36 Bedford Square
London
WC1B 3ES
t + 44 (0)20 7887 4021
f + 44 (0)20 7414 0783

9 781907 896866